SHERPAS

L. S. SUMMER

SMART APPLE MEDIA MANKATO MINNESOTA

Published by Smart Apple Media
123 South Broad Street, Mankato, Minnesota 56001

Produced by The Creative Spark, San Juan Capistrano, CA
    Editor: Elizabeth Sirimarco
    Designer: Mary Francis-DeMarois
    Art Direction: Robert Court
    Page Layout: Jo Maurine Wheeler

Photos/Illustrations: Corbis/Christine Kolisch 4; Corbis/John Noble 6;
Corbis/Allison Wright 7, 12, 18, 19, 20; Kevin Davidson 8; Corbis/Sheldan
Collins 10; Corbis/Craig Lovett 14; Corbis/Hulton-Deutsch Collection 16;
Corbis/David Samuel Robbins 24; Chris Noble/AllStock/PNI 27

Library of Congress Cataloging-in-Publication Data
Summer, L.S., 1959–
    Sherpas / by L.S. Summer.
       p. cm. — (Endangered cultures)
    Includes index.
    Summary: Details the history, culture, and traditional way of life
of the Sherpas, who live in Nepal around Mt. Everest, as well as
their current status and struggle to preserve their culture and identity.
       ISBN 1-887068-95-3 (alk. paper)
       1. Sherpas—Social life and customs—Juvenile literature. [1. Sherpas.]
    I. Title. II. Series.
DS493.9.S5S86 1999
305.895—dc21   98-40020

First edition

9   8   7   6   5   4   3   2   1

Table of Contents

Sherpas live in a beautiful region of Nepal known as Solu-Khumbu, a legendary place of peace and contentment.

High Peaks and Hidden Valleys

Most people long for a place of peace and happiness, where every desire is met, and worries and cares are gone forever. Perhaps it is a faraway island, or a mountain top so high that one can easily hide from the nagging responsibilities of everyday life.

Myths and legends from around the world tell of exactly such a place. Among the people who live in the **Himalayas** of India, Nepal, and Tibet, this magic land is hidden in a remote valley, concealed by high mountains and magical powers. The ancient writings from this region call it the Kingdom of Shambhala, a special place where people live in peace with each other and with the earth. In other countries, people call this land Shangri-La.

For centuries, travelers have searched for this mystical place. Many have visited **Mount Everest,** the world's tallest mountain, in the hope of finding it. This great mountain, located in northeastern Nepal, is part of the Himalayan range.

Mt. Everest is in the heartland of the Sherpas, a group of people who migrated from the Kham region of Tibet

Clans from a region of Tibet called Kham migrate into Nepal, settle in Khumbu, and become known as Sherpas.

The Sherpas have lived in the Himalayas of Nepal for nearly five centuries.

between the 12th and 15th centuries. They traveled west, finally arriving in what is now Nepal in the early 16th century. The word sherpa comes from the Tibetan *shar pa*, which means person from the east. The Sherpas have their own language, also known as Sherpa, which is based on the Tibetan language.

The first Sherpa settlers traveled over a mountain pass called Nangpa La ("la" means "pass" in Tibetan). This pass later became the most important trade route between Nepal and Tibet. The area just below the pass is known as Khumbu—the highest, coldest, and most rugged of the three interconnected regions that form Solu-Khumbu. The Solu area is to the south. Between Solu and Khumbu lies the Pharak valley. The Solu and Pharak areas are home to about 17,000 Sherpas. Approximately 3,000 more live in the rock, ice, and snow of Khumbu.

No one knows for sure why several Tibetan **clans** decided to travel more than one thousand miles and settle in the Solu-Khumbu region. Perhaps they fled the conquering **Mongols,** who had already taken over most of China and were intent on spreading their empire throughout Asia. Fewer than 50 Sherpas probably formed the original group that came to Solu-Khumbu in 1533. As of 1998, approximately 45,000 Sherpas live around the world. Estimates suggest that about 35,000 live in Nepal, and the majority of the rest are spread across India, Bhutan, and Tibet. Several hundred Sherpas live in other nations around the world, particularly in Europe and the United States.

1667

Solu-Khumbu's first Buddhist monastery, called Pangboche, is founded.

Four Sherpa farm workers in the Solu valley stop briefly to rest. Since the Sherpas first arrived in Nepal hundreds of years ago, farming has been an important part of their livelihood.

Nangpa La

Mt. Everest

KHUMBU

Pangboche Monastery

Tengboche Monastery

Namche Bazaar

PHARAK

SOLU

TIBET/CHINA

Lhasa

NEPAL

Delhi

Kathmandu

BHUTAN

Darjeeling

INDIA

BANGLADESH

BURMA

Sherpas As They Were

Two factors influence traditional Sherpa life: the rugged land where they live and the ideals of their religion, Tibetan **Buddhism**. The circle, or *khorlo*, is an important spiritual symbol. Life itself is seen as a circle, where an event results from everything that came before it. The cycle of the seasons, for example, is a *khorlo*, vital to farming and herding—especially in the cold, high-altitude world of the Sherpas.

When the Sherpas first settled in Solu-Khumbu, they lived as farmers and shepherds. The warmer, more southern area of Solu was best for growing crops, such as wheat and barley. The Khumbu area was better for herding yak and dzo, a crossbreed of a cow and a yak that thrives in cold mountain lands.

Sherpa settlements can be found at the highest elevations of any human habitations. In Khumbu, Sherpa villages are located between 10,000 and 14,000 feet (3,050 to 4,270 meters) above sea level. Snow covers the ground from

An estimated 20,000 Sherpas live in the Solu-Khumbu region of Nepal. In the Khumbu region, Sherpas graze livestock, such as yak and dzo. The fertile Solu and Pharak regions supply the Sherpas with ample land to grow crops, including potatoes and barley. Tourists and mountain climbers often visit the Khumbu village of Namche Bazaar, and Khumbu is also the home of two important spiritual centers, the Pangboche and Tengboche Buddhist monasteries.

November through February in Khumbu, and severe weather makes farming and shepherding impossible. The Sherpas of Khumbu solve this problem with a tradition of farming and herding known as **transhumance**. In the winter, they leave the high altitudes to farm in the lower, warmer regions and live in villages with 50 to 100 homes. These homes, built of wood and stone, are usually two stories tall. Goats and calves that cannot survive the cold live on the ground floor.

Summer temperatures in Solu-Khumbu vary according to altitude. At higher altitudes of 11,000 feet (3,350 meters)

Two young Sherpas herd yak calves. The yak is a hardy animal that thrives in the rugged land of Solu-Khumbu.

or more, it never warms much beyond approximately 55°F (12°C)—even in July. Still, the somewhat warmer temperatures allow the Sherpas to graze their herds in these colder, steeper areas. The Sherpas leave their permanent homes and gather in communities called yersa. In the *yersa*, they live in small, simply built huts with stone roofs. As the summer season passes, and temperatures begin to drop, they return again to their villages in the lower valleys. Thus, their way of life is a circle, reflecting the *khorlo*.

In the southern regions of Solu and Pharak, Sherpas grow wheat and barley in the winter, buckwheat and corn in the summer. The potato, introduced in the mid-1900s, has become a dominant crop throughout Solu-Khumbu.

The breeding and herding of animals holds more prestige than farming. The hair of yak and dzo can be made into wool for clothing and blankets. These animals also produce dairy products, especially butter. Butter is used for food, but Tibetan Buddhists also use it to fuel lamps during religious ceremonies. They believe these lamps bring blessings, called **sonam**, to those who light them. They also mix pigment into butter to decorate the ritual cakes known as **torma**.

Yak and dzo were once critical to another aspect of Sherpa life. Sherpas were important traders between Tibet and Nepal. These sturdy animals carried grain up to Tibet from the Nepalese lowlands. The return trip brought salt from Tibet to southern and eastern Nepal. Sometimes they sold or traded the animal's hides and meat in Tibet.

Early Sherpa settlements were made up of 18 clan groups. The Sherpa word for clan is *ru*, which means bone—so called because a Sherpa's clan relationship is

1922

The first attempt to reach the summit of Mt. Everest results in the death of seven Sherpa porters, killed in an avalanche.

SHERPA NAMES

According to Barbara Pijan Lama, Director of the Sherpa Friendship Association in Berkeley, California, there are several ways that Sherpa parents can name their children.

The easiest way is to name the child after the day of the week on which he or she was born. In Tibetan Buddhism, specific planets rule each weekday, and these planets were traditionally worshiped as gods. Each planet protects the children born on the day it rules.

Sherpas may also give children what is known as a Virtue name. Virtues are often embodied in gods and goddesses in

Tibetan Buddhism. For example, a child might be named Wang-chuk, which translates to Power Holder, or Mighty One. Another example is Tshe-ring, which means Long Life. In some instances, the birth day name might be combined with the Virtue name.

Also, a great many Sherpas are called "ang," plus another name. Ang simply means small one or beloved. Thus, a Sherpa might be named Ang Tshe-ring, meaning Beloved Long Life, or Ang Nyi-ma, meaning Beloved Sunday-born.

Sherpa parents normally ask a *lama* (a Buddhist spiritual leader) to name a new baby in a blessing ceremony. Parents often give the child a family name in addition to the *lama* name, so a child may have three or four different names. Sometimes a Sherpa child will be called one name by the mother's relatives and a completely different name by the father's relatives. A Sherpa's name may be changed at any time during his or her life through name-changing ceremonies.

thought to be passed on through the bones. A Sherpa inherits clan identity through his or her father, and Sherpas traditionally choose a spouse from a different clan.

The leaders of Sherpa villages were usually the eldest members of the clans. The villagers followed them because they believed they were wise people who made good decisions. Some legends say that the cooperation of Himalayan mountain lions inspired these leaders.

Sherpas are now considered citizens of Nepal, but in the past, they were independent from the rulers in other parts of Tibet and Nepal. They paid taxes to their own king-like rulers, known as *pembu*. The *pembu* often tried to claim land and political power for themselves. Sometimes to inspire fear, they convinced other Sherpas that they had magical powers.

Now, as in the past, Sherpas live in **nuclear families** much like those of western countries. Each family owns its own land, herds, and personal property. The family has a strong sense of independence, unlike an **extended family**, which is typical of other Asian cultures.

Within the family, a strong ranking system exists—particularly among brothers. There is no word that simply means brother. Instead, there are specific words for older brother, middle brother, and younger brother, used to indicate the order of birth. The oldest brother has the most authority and status, but the youngest has some special privileges of his own, such as inheriting his parent's house after caring for them in old age. Woe to all brothers in the middle, who must fight it out for themselves.

1950

Nepal becomes a constitutional monarchy in which the powers of the ruler are restricted by law.

Mt. Everest is the highest mountain on earth, soaring five and one-half miles (nearly nine kilometers) into the sky. The Tibetans and the Sherpas call it Chomolungma, which means Mother Goddess of the Earth.

Chomolungma

Towering above the Himalayan range at just over 29,000 feet (8,848 meters) is the mountain Tibetans and Sherpas call Chomolungma—Mother Goddess of the Earth. This mountain can be seen from locations in Nepal, India, and Tibet. The Sherpas consider it a sacred place and the home of a powerful female goddess.

Chomolungma is sometimes translated as Lady Goddess of the Wind. The Nepalese call it Sagarmatha, which means Churning Stick of the Ocean. When British government officials surveyed this area in the early 1850s, they called it simply Peak XV. In 1852, it was recognized as the highest peak on earth. Four years later, it became known as Mount Everest, named in honor of Sir George Everest, the head British surveyor.

It was around this time that many Sherpa men moved to Darjeeling, India. Darjeeling was becoming a modern city, attracting tourists from around the world. The idea of traveling for fun and adventure was new. For the first time, people from the United States and Europe could travel long distances to explore faraway countries, thanks to improved forms of transportation.

*Chinese troops
occupy Tibet.*

Sherpas had begun to distinguish themselves as first-rate tour guides. They developed a reputation for hard work, an easy-going manner, and honesty. Since they had lived in the region their entire lives, Sherpas were adapted to high altitudes and could carry heavy loads. Americans and Europeans often employed them to lead expeditions to the most famous mountain of the Sherpa homeland, Mt. Everest.

Tenzing Norgay, a Sherpa guide, led Sir Edmund Hillary to the top of Mount Everest. This photograph was taken in 1953—the year Norgay and Hillary became the first people to reach the summit.

In 1922, a British mountaineering party hired 50 Sherpa **porters,** who carried provisions and led the way on the first attempt to reach the very top, the summit, of Everest. The expedition failed. In the years to come, many more attempts were made to conquer Everest. It was 31 years later, on May 29, 1953, when a Sherpa named Tenzing Norgay and an explorer from New Zealand named Sir Edmund Hillary finally reached the summit. The success of Norgay, along with the other Sherpas on the expedition, helped cement their reputation as indispensable guides and porters. As of 1998, more than 700 hundred climbers had reached the summit of Everest, but 4,000 people had tried. Sherpa guides actually carried a few of those who did succeed to the top.

In 1964, Professor Christoph von Furer-Haimendorf visited Solu-Khumbu. He later published a book that described an idealized Sherpa culture of peace and harmony. More people began to think of the region as the mystical Shangri-La. Only 20 travelers had visited Solu-Khumbu before the book was published. In 1974, more than 3,500 foreign visitors found their way there, and in 1986, more than 6,000 outsiders visited the region. By the late 1990s, more than 400,000 people a year were visiting Nepal, and many of those made Solu-Khumbu their destination.

After the 1950s, most expeditions to Everest were organized in Kathmandu, the capital of Nepal. The Sherpas saw the profit that could be made by leading a **trek** into the mountains. Sherpas were known around the world as the best mountain guides, and the word sherpa became interchangeable with porter.

Mountain climbing holds no fascination in traditional Sherpa culture. To the Sherpas and other Tibetan Buddhists,

1953

Sir Edmund Hillary and Tenzing Norgay reach the Everest summit. The first of the Hillary Schools is built.

Thousands of Tibetan refugees flee to Solu-Khumbu.

all things—people, animals, plants, rivers, lakes, and mountains—are part of the sacred *khorlo*. Each must be respected in its own right. More than 50 Sherpas have died on Mt. Everest since the first expeditions in the early 20th century. Some Sherpas believe such deaths occur because humans violate their sacred relationship with nature when they make a profit leading treks into the mountains.

Sherpas have become popular guides for the many tourists who travel to the Himalayas every year. The challenging treks seem easy for the Sherpa guides, who are agile and swift climbers—even when carrying heavy loads.

MANI RIMDU

As one way to honor the *khorlo*, Sherpas and other Tibetan Buddhists hold celebrations at certain times during the year. The festival of *Mani Rimdu* is held on the full moon of the 10th month of the Tibetan calendar. This festival celebrates Chenresig, a celestial being of great compassion; Guru Rinpoche, an Indian holy man; and other supernatural beings who protect the Everest region.

Over 17 days, the monks make many foods for the celebration, including *rilpu*, which are little red food pellets that bestow good health and blessings. The 16th day is celebrated with magical costumed dances. These dances are the highlight of the festival for the observer but are not merely for show. They are a form of prayer, and each one honors a specific form of wisdom. The festival concludes with a large bonfire on the 17th day, said to purify all negative energies and help all beings let go of the past.

At 12,700 feet (3,871 meters), the monastery of Tengboche, which means Great High Place, has become famous for this ritual and hosts thousands of visitors each year.

Buddhist monks perform a purification prayer at a monastery in Nepal. At one time, one-third of all male Sherpas would spend time at Buddhist monasteries where they would learn to read Tibetan. Many Sherpas no longer speak Tibetan or Sherpa, but only English and Nepali.

Tourists, Trekking, and Change

The popularity of the Solu-Khumbu region as a tourist destination has brought many changes to the Sherpa's world. A successful porter or *sidar* may spend up to 10 months away from the village. Less time is spent with family and friends, and less time can be devoted to traditional religious rituals and community affairs.

Changes in Sherpa education have also had an impact on traditional culture. In 1961, Sir Edmund Hillary and the Himalayan Trust founded a village school system. The Hillary Schools taught classes in Nepali and English, but this meant that fewer people learned Sherpa and Tibetan.

The first teachers at the Hillary Schools were native Sherpas who had been educated in Darjeeling. Others respected them as models of success, but the allure of well-paid trekking jobs soon took them away from teaching. Only non-Sherpa Nepalese remained to teach in the schools. These teachers were not well received in the villages, and many children left the Hillary Schools after a few years.

Another reason many did not finish school is that the long-range value of a good education could not compete with the get-rich-quick lure of the trekking industry. Parents did not encourage their children to remain in school. They thought it was better to become a well-paid *sidar* or tour organizer. By the early 1970s, the few children left in the Hillary schools were actually paid to attend.

Other forces changed the way Sherpas live as well. In the 1950s, the Chinese military occupied Tibet. China had long claimed that Tibet was part of their territory and finally used military force to gain control, killing thousands of Tibetans in the years that followed. Those who survived could no longer practice their religion or traditional way of life. Tibetan refugees fled to the Khumbu valley. The Chinese closed the important Nangpa La trade route between Tibet and Nepal. Trade had been nearly one-third of the Sherpas' total income. The loss of income, together with the greater number of people in the region, increased competition for resources. Sherpas needed to look for new ways to support themselves.

Deforestation has also played a role in the changing world of the Sherpas. As more and more tourists visit Nepal, trees are cut down so the wood can be used as campfire fuel. The traditional cycle of transhumance helped the Sherpas conserve resources, using the majority of fuel only during the winter. Tourists, however, expect fires to be available year-round. The construction of lodges and restaurants for "teahouse trekkers" (those who do not set up camps) has also drained natural resources.

In 1975, the government of Nepal created Sagarmatha National Park in the Khumbu region at the base of Mt. Everest. Its mission is to protect and nurture the forest, wildlife, and natural habitat of the area. Some Sherpas feel the conservation efforts of the park will hurt local residents, who have lived in harmony with the land for centuries. Sherpas fear park officials will control how they graze their livestock and take away land long used to grow crops. They resent the intrusion of the park authority, which was created without any input from Sherpa leaders.

The establishment of Sagarmatha may mean the end of independence for the Sherpas, but it may be a necessary fact of life if the Solu-Khumbu region is to survive the impact of the thousands of tourists who visit each year.

1978

Mountain climbers Reinhold Messner and Peter Habeler become the first people to reach the summit of Mt. Everest without artificial oxygen.

THE LAND OF KHUMBU

The founder of Tibetan Buddhism is known as Guru Rinpoche, which means Precious Teacher. He is held in the highest esteem and was the advisor to many kings. Because of his advanced spiritual powers, his followers believed he could see the future. Guru Rinpoche knew that someday Tibet would be overcome by foreign invaders. He decided to use mystical powers to hide some of the valleys in the Himalayan region as places of refuge for his followers when these dark times arrived. When the Chinese government gained control over Tibet in 1959, many Tibetans fled to the land of Khumbu, where Guru Rinpoche had promised they would find peace.

Sherpas make the high peaks of the Himalayas more accessible to travelers who could not make the trek without their help.

East Meets West

The Solu-Khumbu region is a favorite tourist destination not only because of the rugged beauty of the land, but also because of the Sherpa people. Western travelers like what they have heard about the Sherpas, and many Sherpas are fond of the tourists as well.

A hotel in the tourist town of Namche Bazaar displays pictures of the king and queen of Nepal and the Dalai Lama (the spiritual head of Tibetan Buddhism). Next to these are photographs of the current American president and celebrities like Robert Redford. Fruit trees that are not native to the region grow on the grounds of the Everest View Hotel, built in 1972 by a Japanese businessman. Each tree bears a plaque showing the name of the person who donated it.

Usually prejudice and racism reflect a negative view of another culture, but people can also project a romantic image onto a group of people, preventing a realistic perspective of that group. They cease being individuals and become **stereotypes.** This has happened to the Sherpas, who seem to many foreigners as simple, friendly Nepalese who work

1993

Pasang Lhamu Sherpa becomes the first Sherpa woman to reach the summit of Mt. Everest but dies on the return trip.

as *sidars*, not as people from a rich culture with a long and interesting history. Some outsiders forget that thousands of Sherpas are not guides or porters at all but continue to live as farmers and shepherds.

Have things changed so much in the Solu-Khumbu valley that traditional Sherpa culture is gone? Sherpas themselves believe this is partially true. Tourism has been both good and bad for the Sherpas. The ever-increasing number of people who come to Solu-Khumbu causes problems for the environment. For one thing, when visitors leave their garbage behind, there isn't anywhere to dispose of it, and trash quickly accumulates in makeshift dumps. Problems exist for the Sherpas as well. They depend heavily on outsiders to bring money into their communities. Many things, such as food and cloth, cost more these days. Wealthy Sherpas have left their homes and traditions for the city life in Kathmandu.

To preserve Sherpa traditions and values, the Sherpa Cultural Center has been built at Tengboche Monastery, a popular spot for tourists. It houses a library with books in several languages on the religion, history, and culture of Solu-Khumbu. There is also a museum of traditional Himalayan crafts.

Sherpas outside of Nepal are doing what they can to tell others about their unique culture as well. The United Sherpa Association in New York and the Sherpa Friendship Association in California have been organized by Sherpas living in the United States. These organizations unite the Sherpas of North America and also promote and preserve their traditional way of life.

The Sherpas of the Himalayas are lucky to live in a region so beautiful that people from around the world think of it as the mystical, hidden land called Shangri-La. While this has changed their culture in a number of ways, it has also supplied an additional source of income for the residents of Solu-Khumbu. Into the 21st century, the Sherpas will undoubtedly be guiding tourists high up the remote and mysterious slopes of Mt. Everest. At the same time, agriculture and shepherding survive in Solu-Khumbu. Sherpas continue to practice the rites of their ancient religion and pass on the traditions of their remarkable history to the youngest members of their *ru*.

1996

Eight mountain climbers die on an American expedition to the summit of Mt. Everest.

Tourists often use the village of Namche Bazaar as a base to explore the Himalayan region, but Sherpas consider it the capital of their homeland.

Glossary

Buddhism   The religion that grew from the teachings of the Buddha, a man born into a royal family in sixth-century Nepal who left his kingdom to search for inner peace. The world's third-largest religion, it is practiced in many different forms throughout the world.

clans   Groups of people who trace their descent from a common ancestry.

deforestation   Clearing away forests, usually implying a lack of concern for the ecology of the region.

extended family   A family unit that is made up of not only parents and children, but grandparents, aunts, uncles, and cousins as well.

Himalayas   A mountain range of south-central Asia that is 1,500 miles (2,400 kilometers) long.

Mongols   Warring tribes from what is now Mongolia whose empire stretched across most of Asia between 1200 and 1700.

Mt. Everest   The world's tallest mountain, 29,029 feet (8,848 meters) above sea level.

nuclear families	Family groups made up of two parents and their children.
porters	Individuals employed to carry provisions or baggage.
sidar	The head guide on a trekking expedition.
sonam	Special blessings that Tibetan Buddhists believe are received for doing good deeds.
stereotypes	Standard, overly simple ideas of what something, such as a group of people, is like.
torma	A heavy, flat cake made as a ritual offering among Tibetan Buddhists. Torma can be as small as a muffin or as big as a wedding cake, depending on the size of a ceremony, and are often decorated with colored butter.
transhumance	The custom of seasonally herding livestock to higher or lower pastures.
trek	A trip or journey that often involves difficult traveling conditions.

Further Reading and Information

BOOKS:

Demi. *The Dalai Lama: A Biography of the Tibetan Spiritual and Political Leader.* New York, NY: Henry Holt and Co., 1998.

Heinrichs, Ann. *Nepal (Enchantment of the World Series).* Danbury, CT: Children's Press, 1996.

Pandell, Karen, with Barry Bryant. *Learning from the Dalai Lama: Secrets of the Wheel of Time.* New York, NY: Dutton Children's Books, 1995.

WEB SITES:

http://www.bena.com/Sherpa1/sfa/sFA_home.htm

http://pbs.org/wgbh/nova/everest

Index

Items in bold print indicate illustration.